I Can Read About™
Manatees

Written by Janet Palazzo-Craig • Illustrated by Peter Barrett

Consultant: Daniel K. Odell, Ph.D., Sea World, Inc., Orlando, Florida

Troll

This edition published in 2002.

Illustrations copyright © 1999 by Peter Barrett.
Text copyright © 1999 by Troll Communications L.L.C.

I CAN READ ABOUT is a trademark of Troll Communications L.L.C.

Published by Troll Communications L.L.C.

Printed in the United States of America.   ISBN 0-8167-4718-0

10 9 8 7 6

Look closely—what do you see? What is that shadowy shape moving slowly through the water? This gentle creature is called a *manatee* (MAN-uh-TEE).

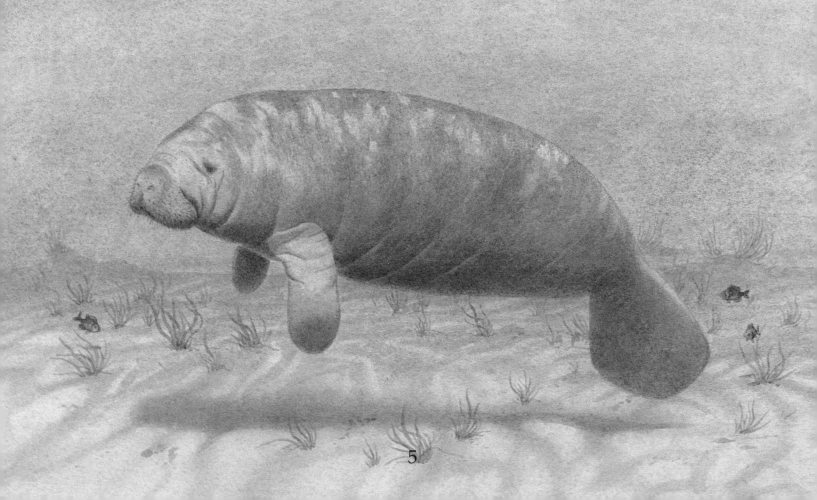

Slowly, the manatee swims through the shallow water, grazing on sea grass. It uses one of its flippers to push the plants to its mouth. The manatee must eat a lot to keep itself alive. When there is plenty of food, it may eat 100 pounds (45 kilograms) of plants a day.

Manatees are big! An average one weighs about 1,500 pounds (680 kilograms) and grows to a length of 10–14 feet (3–4 meters). The manatee's thick skin is gray or grayish-brown.

Manatees are sometimes called sea cows. Like a cow, the manatee grazes on grass. But the manatee's diet is the grass that grows *under* the water.

There are three types of manatees. One is the West Indian manatee. It is found in the warm waters of Florida, in the Caribbean Sea, and along the coast of South America.

West Indian manatee

Another type of manatee is the African manatee. It lives in the rivers and coastal waters of western Africa.

African manatee

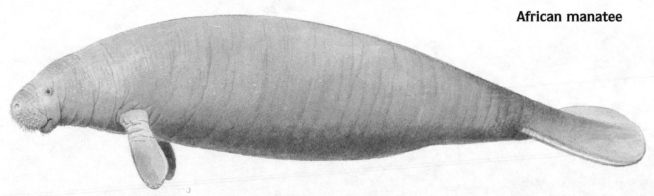

Amazon manatee

The third is the Amazon manatee, which lives in the Amazon River of South America. This creature is the only manatee that spends all its time in fresh water. Other manatees can live in both fresh and salt water.

The Amazon manatee is also different in another way. It is the only manatee that does not have nails on its flippers.

Locations of manatees throughout the world

Manatees belong to a group of animals called *Sirenia* (sy-REE-nee-uh). This name comes from the word *siren*. Ancient Greek legends tell of sirens, female creatures who lived in the sea. It was said that the sirens sang beautiful songs that lured sailors to their death in rocky waters.

How did these legends begin? Perhaps, long-ago sailors had never seen a manatee before, so they tried to get a closer look. Did these sailors crash their boat on the rocks, beginning the legend of the sirens?

Stories of mermaids may also be based on manatee sightings. Of course, manatees are not really mermaids or sirens. A manatee is a *mammal*, a warm-blooded creature that nurses its young with milk from the mother's body.

Being warm-blooded means that a mammal's body temperature stays about the same, no matter how hot or cold the surrounding temperature is. Cold-blooded animals, such as snakes and fish, are different. Their body temperatures change along with the surrounding air or water.

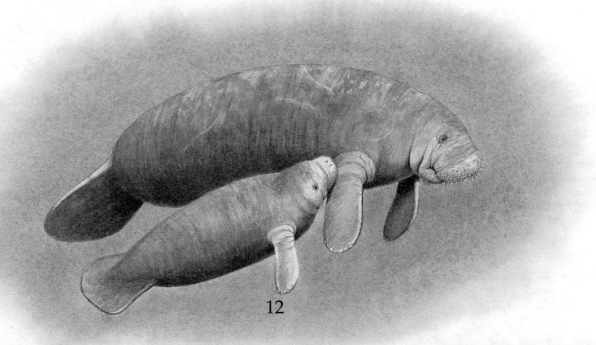

Like other mammals, manatees have hair. These bristles are scattered over the manatee's body. The manatee also has whiskers around its mouth and nose. These whiskers serve as feelers for finding food along the sandy sea bottom.

Scientists think the manatee's closest living relatives are the elephant and a rabbit-sized rodent called a *hyrax*. This means that, millions of years ago, these three creatures shared the same ancestor.

The manatee's ancestor had four legs, lived on land, and ate plants. Although plants still make up its diet, the manatee *adapted,* or changed, over the course of several million years. About sixty million years ago, the manatee became a marine mammal. It left land to spend all its life in the water.

Skeleton of modern-day manatee

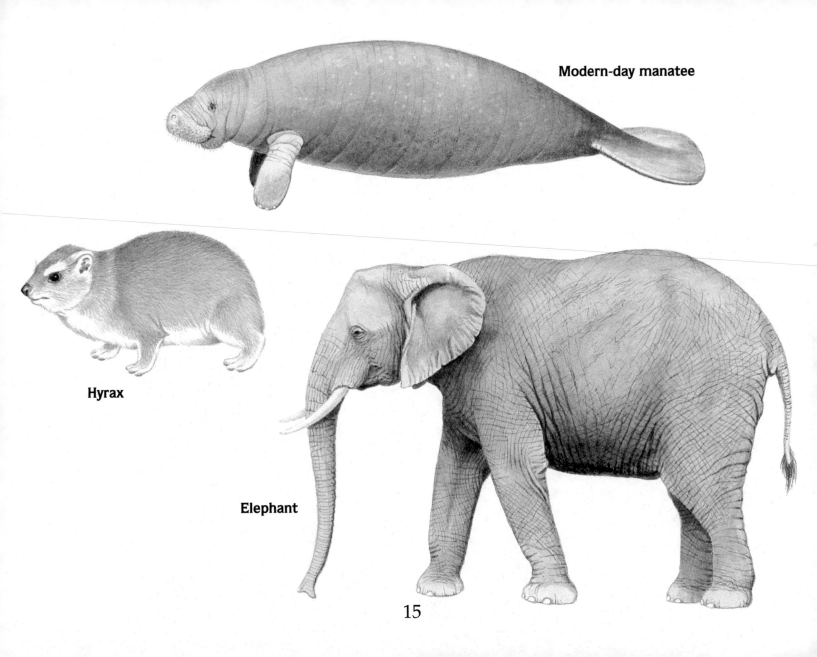

Modern-day manatee

Hyrax

Elephant

15

The manatee's body *evolved*—it gradually developed and changed to suit life in the water. The manatee lost its legs. The front legs became flippers. The back legs disappeared. A powerful, paddle-shaped tail developed to help the manatee swim.

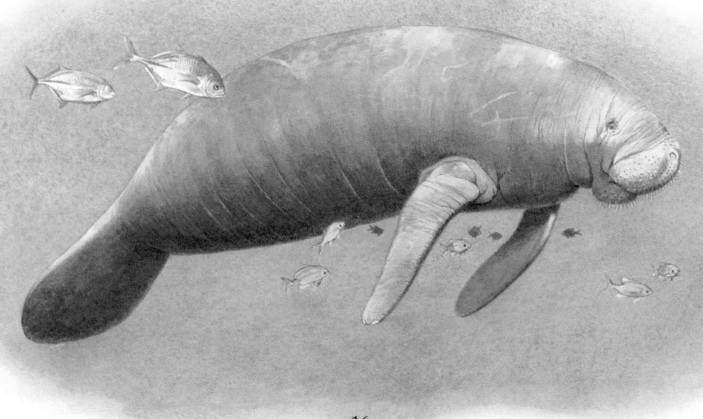

The manatee adapted to life in the water in other ways, too.
Like other mammals, the manatee has lungs for breathing air.
It must come to the surface of the water to breathe. So the manatee
developed special nostrils that clamp shut tightly to keep water out
when the manatee is underwater. These "trap-door" nostrils quickly
open for air when the manatee surfaces.

Nature has given the manatee many other special characteristics to help it survive. For example, this creature's upper lip is split into two parts. The two halves work together like a pair of pliers, pulling and tearing at tasty water plants.

The manatee's eyes see well underwater. Manatees do not have eyelids. Each eye is surrounded by a circle of muscles, which closes tightly when the manatee is sleeping.

Manatees can hear well, but they do not have ears on the outside of their bodies. Instead, they have two tiny ear holes. These holes are located behind the manatee's eyes.

Manatees can make many different sounds. Studies suggest that each sound has a special meaning. A high, piercing scream means a manatee is scared. Male manatees looking for females make soft grunting sounds. And every mother manatee can identify her baby by the sound of its cry.

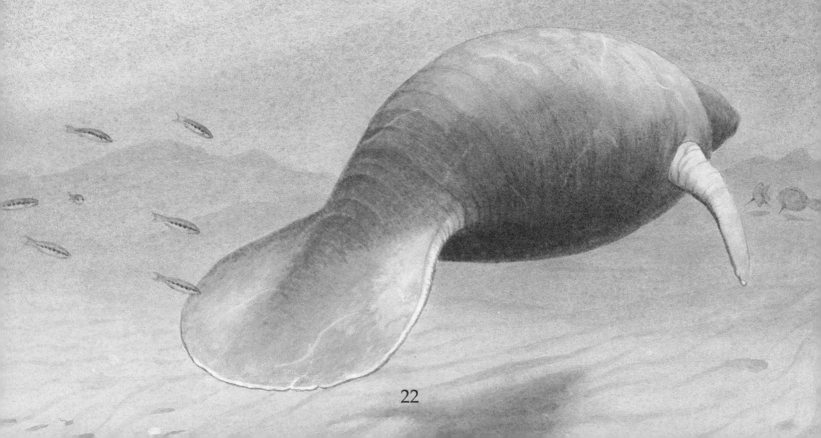

Some scientists believe manatees have another way of communicating with one another, through something called *smell-taste.* Here is how it is thought to work. Special glands on the manatee's body create a variety of scents. If a female is ready to mate, she may rub her scent glands against a rock. Males that pass by the rock can detect the female's scent by smell-tasting it. They receive the message that the female is looking for a mate, and they begin to search for her.

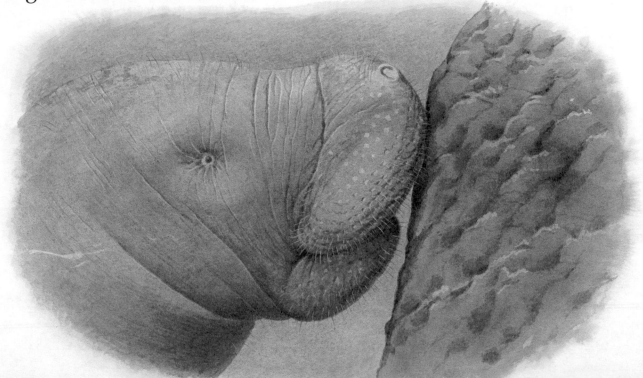

It is believed by some scientists that manatees also may use smell-taste to help them find their way in the dark. Perhaps they smell-taste how much salt and other materials are in the water to follow a "trail" home.

Did you know manatees have special "traveling" teeth to help them eat? A manatee's mouth contains a set of molars, which are big teeth used for grinding plant food. There are four rows of molars—two rows on top and two on the bottom of the jaw. Each row has six or seven teeth.

Many of the water plants that make up the main diet of the West Indian manatee contain a gritty substance called *silica*. Little by little, the silica grates against the manatee's molars and wears them out. But that is not a problem for the manatee! The worn-out teeth move forward in a line and eventually fall out. Meanwhile, in the back of the animal's mouth, new molars have formed. The new teeth travel forward to take the place of the old ones.

Skeleton

Manatees may live as long as sixty years. They spend most of that time alone, wandering through shallow water in search of food.

But at certain times, groups of manatees do gather. During winter, herds of manatees come together in the warm waters of the Crystal River in Florida. This is because manatees must live in water that is warmer than 68 degrees Fahrenheit (20 degrees Celsius). When the ocean water along the coast cools during winter, the manatees head upriver. There, warm springs provide the higher water temperatures and abundant food these animals need to survive. This sort of seasonal journey to and from warm areas is called a *migration*.

When they're together, the manatees enjoy nuzzling and playfully bumping into one another. Their "games" are always friendly. These peaceful creatures have never been observed fighting among themselves or with other animals.

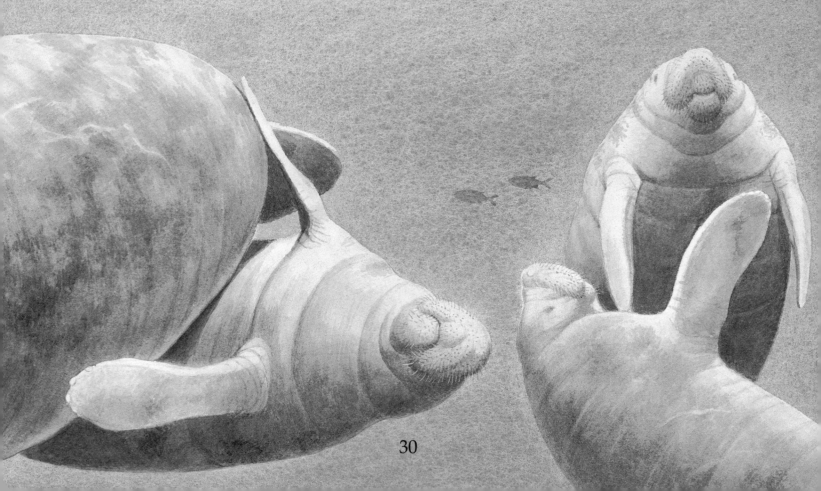

Manatees also gather when a female is ready to mate. After mating, the males do not stay with the females to help raise the young. The mother manatee gives birth after about twelve months of pregnancy.

A baby manatee is called a *calf*. It has a very close relationship with its mother. During the baby's first two years of life, it follows its mother everywhere, learning how to survive.

The baby and mother chatter, squeak, and squeal to each other. This is their way of finding each other at all times. Often, the calf playfully rides on its mother's back or rests on her tail.

When the calf is first born, the mother nurses it with her milk. Then, when it is a few weeks old, the baby adds underwater grass to its diet.

If danger is near, the mother may swim in front of the calf to protect it. But a mother manatee has never been observed fighting with another animal, even to save her baby.

Because they are shy and gentle, manatees are easy prey. They have been hunted by humans for their meat and hides. It is believed that there used to be large numbers of manatees and that they are not as plentiful as they once were. Scientists estimate that in Florida there are about 2,500 manatees.

To help protect manatees, laws now forbid hunting these creatures. But the slow-moving manatee faces many other dangers from people.

The most serious danger to the manatee is the risk of being injured by speeding boats and by boat propellers. That is because manatees live in water that is only 3–10 feet (1–3 meters) deep. Often, boaters do not spot manatees in the water until it is too late. As the boats zoom along, the unlucky manatees are hit by the boats or are cut by their sharp propellers.

These accidents are so frequent that almost all Florida manatees have scars from propellers on their backs and tails. Scientists are even able to identify certain manatees by their unique scars.

Another serious danger to the manatees is the loss of their natural *habitat*, the area in which they live. As people build new homes and industries in places that were once wild, the manatees suffer.

Housing developments often bring litter and pollution, which destroy the underwater grass and plants that manatees eat. Without enough food, the manatees cannot survive.

To make matters worse, mother manatees give birth only once every two to five years. So the manatee birth rate cannot keep up with the numbers that are lost because of pollution and boating accidents.

So few manatees are left that they are considered *endangered*. This means that unless their numbers increase, manatees may become extinct, as the dinosaurs did.

But many people have been working to help manatees survive. New laws have been passed to protect these peaceful creatures. Certain areas have been set aside for the manatees. Boating and industrial development are not allowed in these places.

In Florida, there are special centers to care for injured manatees. Other scientists study the bodies of dead manatees to collect information about these special animals. In another program, researchers attach harmless radio tags to the manatees' tails. The radio signals show the scientists exactly where the manatees swim, rest, and feed.

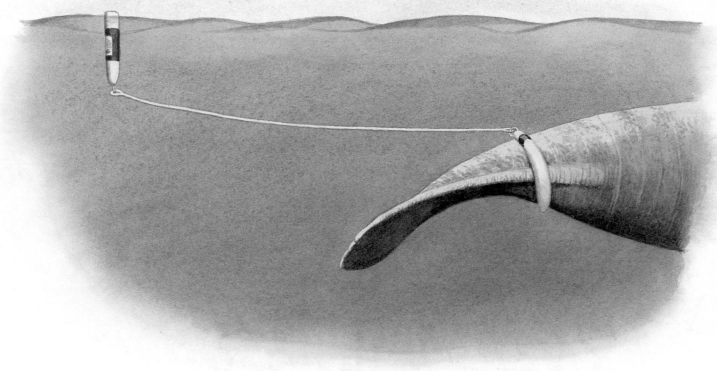

Concerned people hope that efforts to save the manatee will be successful. For this fascinating animal offers much to appreciate and observe in the wonderful world of nature.

Index